D1391940

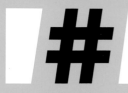

# MILLENNIAL PROBLEMS

**EVERYDAY STRUGGLES OF A GENERATION**

**ROWAN DOBSON**

Illustrations by Marcus Walters
Design by Jesse Holborn

**◙ SQUARE PEG**

1 3 5 7 9 10 8 6 4 2

Square Peg, an imprint of Vintage,
20 Vauxhall Bridge Road,
London SW1V 2SA

Square Peg is part of the Penguin Random House group of companies
whose addresses can be found at global.penguinrandomhouse.com

Text copyright © Square Peg 2017

First published by Square Peg in 2017

Penguin.co.uk/vintage

A CIP catalogue record for this book is available from the British Library

ISBN 9781910931868

Designed by Jesse Holborn
Illustrated by Marcus Walters

Printed and bound by L.E.G.O. S.p.A.

Penguin Random House is committed to a sustainable future for our
business, our readers and our planet. This book is made from Forest
Stewardship Council® certified paper.

# CONTENTS

# INTRO

**I know, I get it,** life's turning out to be as easy as *The Sims* without the cheat codes.

When you're not defending yourself against the latest 'news' article about how millennials are a **bunch of lazy, whiny moaners**, you're checking your bff's Snap and Insta stories to see if they've been passive aggressively attacked via a gif.

Your attempts to find true love through a medium that values looks over ANYTHING and EVERYTHING fail because all you want is for someone to appreciate your hilarious retro nineties references and ironic use of acronyms. #HYD?*

Your efforts to live-tweet alongside the latest debate get interrupted when the **50 pugs you follow** on Twitter all start talking to each other and your pug fomo *always* takes over. #PFFL.**

Your mornings begin in a post-Netflix-binge haze, so you order brunch at the closest **pick-me-up pop-up**, but so often the avo toast is totally uninstagrammable and your soy gluten-free latte is tepid. TSIRz.***

Luckily, our generation has a sense of humour and countless means of sharing it, so I've compiled a few of our most challenging **day-to-day woes**.

**You**, my friend, are not alone.

\* How *You* Doin'?
\*\* Pug Fests For Lyf.
\*\*\* The Struggle is Realz.

# I have a very difficult time spelling millennial

**#millennialproblems**
**#toomanydoubleletters**

# !#
# FOOD

# TFW* you take a single bite of your brunch and instantly experience the overwhelming realisation that *you* will **never ever**, under any circumstances, own a home.

* This footnote is for any oldies perusing the 'young persons' section of the bookshop. HEY OLDIES! PLEASE BUY THIS BOOK WITH ALL YOUR EXTRA CASH**.
TFW = That feeling when.
** This footnote is for any eagle-eyed millennials. CASH is not an acronym, but something people exchanged for things like cars and sofas – things *you* will never own outright. It's a bit like contactless, but with paper. I know, sounds weird. It's hard to explain, but here's an emoji that might help: 💷🖼️

# Tfw your avocado isn't ripe enough #feelsbadman

@eryngo_bragh – 28 Jul

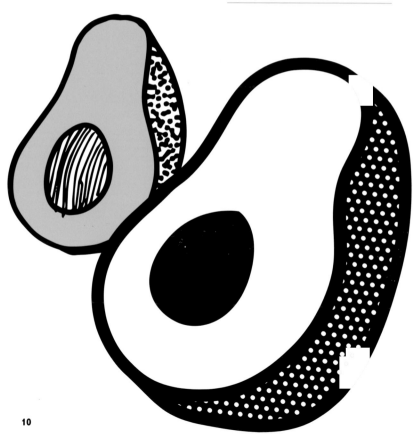

It's always the things you love most that hurt you the hardest.
#atetoomuchavocado
#stomachache
#millennialproblems
#whyimpoor

# WHO DO I HAVE TO FUCK TO GET A BRUNCH SPOT NEXT TO MY AIRB&B?!

I cut my finger slicing open an avocado and now I can't fix my topknot.

**BEING A MILLENNIAL IS EATING AVOCADO TOAST TO DISTRACT YOURSELF FROM THE CRUSHING FEAR FOR THE FUTURE OF OUR DYING PLANET.**

# Every time I eat brunch I think of all the houses I could be buying if I just didn't order the Avocado Toast app.

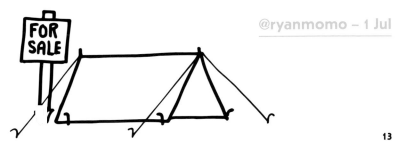

13

# Where is the beetroot emoji when you need it? #FirstWorldProblems

@Garrett_Leigh – 10 Jul

I meant to Snapchat my breakfast but I ate it too fast

@SerAnndipity – 25 Jun

# 'This brunch didn't look good enough to instagram'

# #MillennialFood

# Gluten free organic water.

@Eddie_Writer17 – 22 Jun

# #MillennialFood

# VEGAN UNICORN WATER.

@kennethhuber – 22 Jun

I had to look up how to spell 'casserole' but spelled 'quinoa' without issue.

@comicsemz – 15 Jul

# Finally realised why I can't afford a house it's this delicious $25,364 hipster coffee 6x a day #genY #saynotoavocado

19

# FOR DINNER I HAD CHICKEN NUGGETS AND ICE CREAM. 5 YEAR OLD ME WOULD BE SO PROUD

# Here's my (un)fortune I got. #Savage #fortunecookie

*Blessed are the children for they shall inherit the national debt.*

*Lucky # 10, 16, 38, 39, 41*

21

I think the
real reason
#Millennials
love #brunch
is because
sometimes we
can't afford
to eat both
breakfast
& lunch.😂😭

# FOUND THE STEM NUBBIN OF AN AVOCADO ON MY BED.

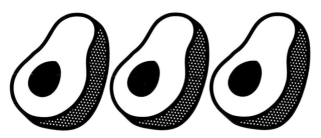

# #SOCIAL

**If you didn't post about it... did it really happen?**

**Friend A:** Shall I 'check in' or do people not do that anymore? Maybe I'll post a pic and tag us both or do you think I should add a caption? Hmmm but what would the caption say? Wait, I'll just put this emoji... But I kinda want to add something off the cuff... something clever, but not too wanky, just something a bit different that also fits into the defined parameters of social expectations... Hold on, I'll see if I drafted any posts in my notes like way back when we booked our tickets. I know I posted about it when I was thinking about going... and then last week I put how much I was looking forward to today, did you see that? And then I posted that selfie on the train this morning, did you see that too? Whatever, doesn't matter, I just *need* to post that I've arrived and I'm having loads of fun, but not in a showy-off way just in a y'know, 'I'm here and have a social life' kind of way and a 'I'm totally happy with how my life is at this moment in time' vibe. So shall I just post a pic? Do you think we can fit the inflatable unicorn in? If the unicorn doesn't fit then there's not much point in a pic... Maybe I'll just 'check in' because that's kind of retro, isn't it?

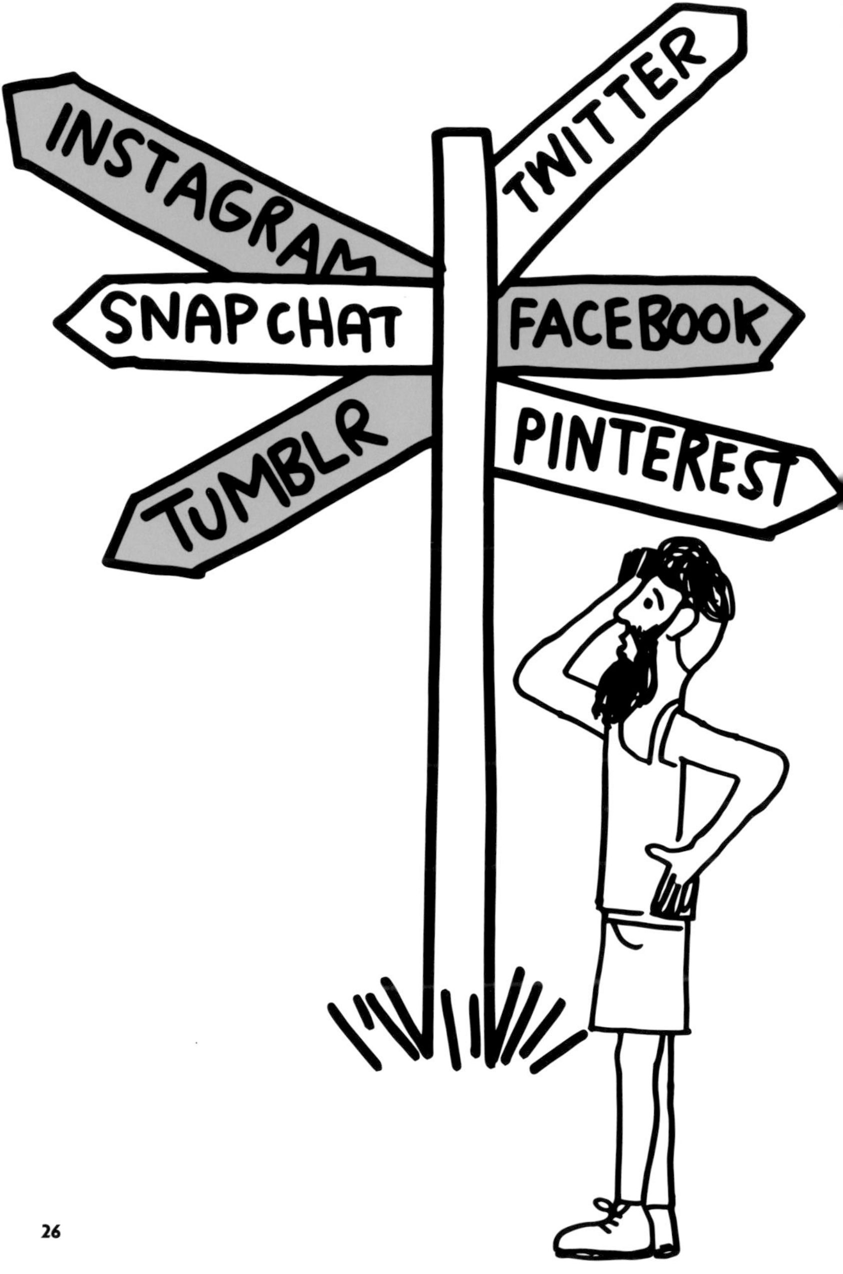
INSTAGRAM
TWITTER
SNAPCHAT
FACEBOOK
TUMBLR
PINTEREST

# Matching Snapchat and Instagram stories are getting to me... choose your medium

@eleprior – 2 Jul

**@instagram is down. If my followers don't know what I'm eating, do I truly exist?? #instagramexistentialism**

@ReturnOfTheVoss – 16 May

Created and purchased a custom @snapchat geofilter for my wedding #somillennial

@SarahElizNev – 18 Oct

# I CAME TO TWITTER TO COMPLAIN ABOUT INSTAGRAM BEING TOO MUCH LIKE SNAPCHAT

@marcel_emerson – 2 Aug

I JUST WITNESSED A MARRIAGE PROPOSAL THROUGH INSTAGRAM LIVE AND IT WAS BEAUTIFUL 💍 😭

Dealing with the confusion of our distant acquaintances changing their last names on Facebook after marriage #millennialproblems

@maggiebutler7 – 20 Jun

**When you're mad at someone so you ignore them but you have a 100+ day snapstreak you don't want to mess up** 😭

@dmedina1994 – 16 Mar

I hate my long hair so much but I can't bear to cut it short because it looks so good on social media

@thesophiachang – 8 Jul

# PHONE BROKE. YESTERDAY WAS UNDOCUMENTED.

for the record I do NOT understand the trend of recently married gals changing their insta username to @mrs*newlastname* #cringe

I like when Facebook reminds me for two weeks about my friendship anniversary w/ that guy who stopped returning my texts.

DAT MOMENT WHEN PEOPLE HAVE 'SEEN' YOUR INVITE ON FB BUT DECIDE NOT TO CLICK GOING, MAYBE OR NO. #MAKETHECHOICEPEEPS

When you accidentally poke someone on FB #mybad #itsnot2008 #whyistherestillpoking

**Sending a friend request you didn't mean to send out on social media**

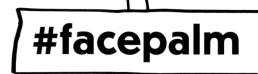

#facepalm

# I plan my adventures around the Instagram captions in my head 🙇

# I HAVE THIS STRANGE DESIRE TO TELL PEOPLE ALL THE LITTLE NOTHINGS IN MY LIFE #TWITTER 🐦 #SNAPCHAT #IMAMILLENNIAL

@wren_thebird – 22 May

Not enough characters to change to my new double barreled surname on #twitter 🐦 #mrs

@BethanyArmorel – 13 Apr

# #millennialproblems

'*I'm sorry I didn't answer my phone when you called. I don't use it for that*'

nothing makes me more irrationally angry than when I can't find the emoji I need. 😬😬😬

# IF I HAVE TO SEE ONE MORE INSTAGRAM OF A DAMN UNICORN FLOATIE ...🦄

# Going to a concert and not being allowed to use snapchat is lowkey torture

When you spend twenty minutes trying to figure out a Twitter debate and then you realize you don't give a shit

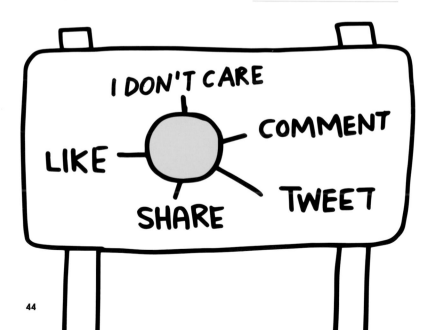

**TRIED TO DEACTIVATE TWITTER BUT THEN THE VMAs HAPPENED #NEVERMIND #MUSTPARTICIPATE**

@HannahLeisman – 30 Aug

**Hate when youre mad at someone but you still wanna send them some good quality memes #toomuchpride**

@evabrownie321 – 4 Apr

# I FORGOT TO PUT 'LOL' AT THE END OF THAT TWEET AND NOW IT LOOKS TOO SERIOUS

# I haven't Instagrammed a selfie or a cat in like two days. #growth

@Alyssapotamus – 18 Jan

BRB, spending the rest of the day trying to decide if I was passively aggressively attacked via a #GIF

@elizahhhhhhope – 6 Jul

# WHEN YOU PUT THE WRONG EMOJI AT THE END OF A RISKY TEXT #MILLENIALPROBLEMS

@AdevaMcG92 – 7 Jun

# Sometimes You Just Need To Read Some Inspirational Quotes On Pinterest.

'*Don't Count the Days – Make the Days Count!*'

'*If You Stumble, Make it Part of the Dance!*'

'*Don't Look Back, You're Not Going That Way!*'

@akuno_101 – 23 Jul

49

# #
# ADULTING

**Have you** eaten actual breakfast food instead of cold pizza from two nights ago?

**Have you** gone out for brunch in a white t-shirt and returned with zero food stains in sight?

**Have you** cooked a whole bunch of healthy stuff from that Buzzfeed article you saw and split it all into Tupperware for the week?

**Welcome to adulting!***

*It's you becoming everything you never thought you would be. And it's shit.

# ADULTING IS POOPY

@DeadWafflez – 2 Jul

I just had to order my takeout OVER THE PHONE because the online ordering service was down. I'm still recovering.

@celena_gentry – 8 Mar

# How do you get red wine stain out of a pug? #adulting

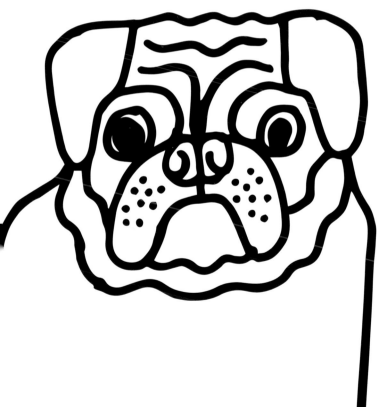

# Adulting is literally the biggest pile of wank 🙄

have to do a food shop later and so far my list includes prosecco, maltesers, crisps and milk #adulting

@chazstockton – 1 Aug

I was just targeted for an AD on Instagram to freeze my eggs. Is this #adulting?

**I CAN REMEMBER THE LYRICS FROM EVERY 90s COUNTRY SONG, BUT I FORGET EVERY DAMN PASSWORD I EVER MAKE.**

*gets home early*
*needs to shower and sleep*
*spends forever sitting in my underwear reading twitter* #adulting

# When you go into WHSmith for glue and spend £40 on colourful pens

@emilyleemusic – 10 Jul

58

# Sometimes there's no better high than cancelled plans. #adultlife

# I just realized I browse LinkedIn more than Facebook now #adulting

Me: When I'm an adult I'm—
Person: Wait aren't you in your 20s?
Me: Shit...
#millennialmoment

**CAN WE JUST APPRECIATE THE FACT THAT I WENT OUT IN A WHITE SHIRT AND I HAVE ZERO STAINS.**

# #
# OLD
# PEOPLE

CAN YOU HEAR ME?

**Yes of course**, I'll explain how to reset the wifi for the 7000th time.

**Yes of course**, I'll smile politely at your 'millennials are whiny, entitled brats' comment.

**Yes of course**, I'll scan that document for you because you 'never *can* remember' the right button to press. (The green one. Always the green one.)

# BUT WILL YOU PLEASE ACKNOWLEDGE THAT EVERYTHING AND I MEAN E V E R Y T H I N G IS MORE DIFFICULT FOR MY GENERATION THAN IT EVER WAS FOR YOURS?

Thank you, glad we cleared that up. Now, a hashtag is...

There's always that one family member who sends one too many Facebook game requests. #comeonnow #itsnot2008

# JUST SPENT 1 HOUR TEACHING MY DAD HOW TO SCAN A PIECE OF PAPER AND SEND IT VIA EMAIL

# I was just scolded for not folding my sweatshirts correctly. In my room. That I share with no one.

@AnnaJKozak – 17 Feb

#MillennialMistake No.1034: Commenting on an older relative's Facebook post. Side effects may include constant & unnecessary notifications.

**MOM: SO WHERE DO YOU TYPE A HASHTAG? DAD: IS THERE LIKE A HASHTAG WEBSITE OR SOMETHING?** 😂

# Tfw parents have just rediscovered tetris and are now addicted to it... and when I tlk to them they dont reply #feelsbadman

@samanthango_ – 31 Jan

Professor hooked up a personal laptop to the projector and keeps getting FarmVille notifications. #2000AndLate

@AnnaJKozak – 17 Feb

# Fucking middle aged people chatting about minecraft on the train #killmenow

@wanklol – 27 Jun

**TFW your 70-year-old mother asks if there is an 'emote Khan' that means 'up yours' and you send her the middle finger emoji** 😐

Mum: My phone's not working, can you fix it?
Dad: The internet won't come on, can you look at the computer?

# MY DAD ORDERS CDs OFF AMAZON #2000ANDLATE

# #FINDING LOVE ♥

If music be the food of love,
DM her your favourite song,
Or link it to your profile,
So she can sing along.

If art reveals the truest soul,
Filter that dodgy selfie,
Tense those abs, insta your brunch,
She'll think you're super healthy.

If IRL is super awks,
Will you meet again?
Or lose your Snapchat streak,
And later click 'unfriend'?

But then she shares her wifi,
Tells people you're together,
Adds you to her Netflix,
Will this last forever?

There's just one way to find out,
Your time is fast approaching,
But ne'er forget that lifeline,
...There is always ghosting...

# WHERE'S MY #WEMETONTWITTER SOULMATE?

@ken_arri – 10 Jul

I finally got this guy's wifi password so I guess you could say things are getting pretty serious. #millennialdating

'*Yeah, sure, my password is: PL3A53 LØV3 M3*'

# Friday nights are for Instagram stalking your ex and accidentally liking a pic from a year ago.

👍 👍 👍

@RyanBalthazor1 – 3 Mar

Idk why they don't call #tinder #plentyoffish, i've never seen so many pictures of guys holding dead fish in my whole life 🐟

# I HAD A #TINDERDATE WHO READ MY ENTIRE #BLOG. HE SAID, 'YOUR LIFE IS AN OPEN BOOK AND I ALREADY READ IT.' 😳#CAUGHT #VULNERABLE #WRITERSLIFE

I've just been asked out for a drink on LinkedIn... Is this a thing?! #awks

Can we just discuss the fact that relationships probably ended because WhatsApp died for 2 hours? 😕 😟

## WHEN YOU ACCIDENTALLY SWIPE LEFT TO YOUR FUTURE WORLDIE HUSBAND #TOOQUICK #TINDERPROBLEMS 😩 🔥

Awkward when people break up and their entire Instagram account is of them and their partner  #deletedelete! #awk

Why can't I super-nope someone on tinder #tinderfails #burnallyourcamo #cargopantstoo #moderndating

@HelenabadgerDGF – 15 Jul

# HE WIPED AWAY HER TEARS AND ACCIDENTALLY HER EYEBROWS TOO

@AdelG9 – 15 Jun

# #moderndating 'will you be my girlfriend' achievement levels

1) let's stop swiping
2) deleting dating apps together
3) Facebook official

@Drkittybee – 28 Jun

Guys, I'm trying to be trusting, but geez, EVERY GUY on @bumble_app cannot be a pilot! #ModernDating

@CNHarder – 30 Jun

## WHEN GIRLS HAVE A FILTER ON EVERY TINDER PIC 😩👎😂

@Samlee1991 – 18 Jul

# #MILLENNIALPROBLEMS THAT AWKWARD CONVERSATION ABOUT WHETHER OR NOT YOU WANT TO BE IN A POLY OR MONO RELATIONSHIP.

@ItsAstridEh – 10 Jul

When you drop your phone and accidentally superlike someone on Tinder #TinderProblems

@JamieTimmy – 17 Jul

# She followed me back on Instagram after 2 months of not talking... Is this a sign from God?

@allenjpatrick55 – 12 Dec

# #

# LITERALLY DYING

Have you ever died?
I mean, actually, properly
died?

As in, a friend has sent
you a meme and it's so
friggin relatable that you've
just stopped functioning
and the grim reaper has
appeared behind you
with a wry smile and an
unexpected resemblance
to Ralph Fiennes (weird,
right?) and you've just
stopped breathing because
you've physically, spiritually,
emotionally, literally died?

Yeah . . . me too.

My biggest fear is becoming a Buzzfeed clickbait story because of a spider crawling into my ear. #sendhelp

@Anna_Merriman – 9 Jul

# OVERHEARD ON THE TRAIN: 'IF I LOSE MY SNAPCHAT STREAKS, MY LIFE WILL BE OVER' 😂

@steph_lawrie – 1 Jun

Going without my phone for a month has really shown me how much of a millennial I am. #dying 😩

@kaywinter_ 3 Jul

I feel like
I can't
biologically
handle a 3
hour class
#literallydying

# instagram
# twitter
# facebook
# instagram
# twitter
# facebook
# #idie

I JUST REALIZED FRED WEASLEY SAYS, 'NO ONE'S DIED RECENTLY' WHEN EXPLAINING QUIDDITCH TO HARRY, BUT HE ENDS UP DYING IN BOOK 7. #FEELSBADMAN

When someone on the bus gets a phone call and their ringer is the same tone as your alarm #literaldeath💀💀💀

@CaitlinCWilson – 26 Jul

**Note to self: Don't ever go 4 days without caffeine/coffee again. #LiteralDeath**

@OliviaKCiotti – 31 Jul

# my body hates me so much after every festival 😭#dying

# N·) NO, NO BREAKDOWNS HERE ABOUT THE FᴀCT THAT DAD CᴀN'T REMEMBER HIS LOGIN FOR S;Y GO AND GoT IᏟ IN LESS THAN 24 H·)URS🙂🙂🙂 #TOTALLIE #DYING

Was sitting on the floor watching TV, and my dog just went underneath my arm to cuddle. #idied #imdeadnow

# SOMEONE JUST ACTUALLY EXCLAIMED AS THEIR CAKE FELL – OH MOTHER HUBBARD! #SOBRITISH #IDIED

Literally doing homework and my dad sends me a picture of him in an elf hat #literallydied #lmao

@Bridget_2510 – 15 Nov

I mean I'll probably have to have a roommate in my grave.

# #
WERK
WERK
WERK

# Welcome to the world of work! Thanks to technological advancements of the past two decades, you will **never** have to **switch off** from this moment forward!

#goodbyefreedom

Am I the only one who has zero time for the beach or pools or any type of summer fun? #werkwerkwerk

@car0linebrewer – 21 Jun

I'm too young to be involved in this sinister office politics made up by menopausal women. #FML

## SHOWS SOMEONE HOW TO MAKE A DESKTOP SHORTCUT. BECOMES TECH GUY.

How am I supposed to study for my exam when the 50 pugs I follow on twitter are all talking to each other & sharing the h*cking cutest pics

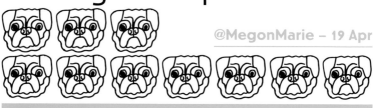

@MegonMarie – 19 Apr

# PEOPLE WHO RESPOND TO MY EMAILS BY CALLING ME ARE PURE EVIL.

@AmandaMarie_19 – 11 Jul

# With a Bachelor's in Bullshit and a Master's in Google Search, one can achieve anything.

## #BeingAMillennial #GenerationY

Eating Coco Puffs, watching Netflix and waiting for a conference call from the boss man in my pjs. It's almost noon. #winninglife

I wonder if my boss
has noticed I wear
the same shoes every
day...#brokemillennial
#mydogeatsmyshoes

## JUST CONFUSED NOVEMBER RAIN FOR PURPLE RAIN AND MY COWORKER GOT MAAAAAD.

# SOMETIMES IT'S A LEGIT STRUGGLE FOR ME NOT TO PUT A SMILEY FACE EMOTICON INTO A PROFESSIONAL EMAIL.

# If I could describe my first year of working in two words it would be: generational gap

When you're one of three employees under the age of 30, you're automatically a tech genius

## JUST GAVE THE EXEC DIRECTOR A TWITTER 101 CRASH COURSE. #IMAMILLENNIAL

@sweeneywi – 18 Nov

I have a long day ahead of me. I left my headphones at home. Now I have to listen to people at work.

@SpencerMorris13 – 16 Dec

# Just asked my boss what side a stamp goes on a letter being mailed

That awkward moment
ur boss walks up behind
u as you're not only
on Facebook but also
scrolling thru pictures
of urself ♥60

# IT'S COOL I.T. I'LL FIX MY IMAC ALL BY MYSELF

# #PLUGGED IN

**Wake up**. Check what you look like on Snapchat. Add a **filter** to make yourself look cute. **Send snap** – 'Just woke up, 08.38.' Check Twitter. **Check** Instagram. **Tag** friend in a hilarious meme on Facebook – 'omg this is so us I am crying [insert crying with laugher emoji]' – you are not crying with laughter. **Spotify playlist on**, get ready, **post tweet** – 'I need coffee ASAP [insert coffee emoji]' – you don't even like coffee. **Headphones on**. Avoid everyone on public transport. Get to work, spend whole morning on WhatsApp. **Order** Deliveroo at lunch because you cba to socialise IRL. **Watch** that funny video your friend sent to the group chat. 17.30, **send text** to friends – 'Sorry guys I'm so wiped, had such a busy day, can't make drinks but brunch this weekend?' – you aren't really that tired. **Headphones on**. Avoid everyone on public transport. Get home, **send snap** of your kale couscous balsamic vinegar dinner – 'Health kick starts now guys!!' – then eat a whole packet of digestives. **Binge on Netflix**. Resist the temptation to **live-tweet** your reactions so your friends don't think you bailed on them to watch Netflix in your room, on your own. **Again**.

Set alarm, **snooze alarm**, repeat.

# @APPLE HUMANITY CAN'T SURVIVE WITHOUT A DABBING EMOJI. YOU REALLY NEED TO CREATE ONE ASAP.

@samhooker10 – 19 Dec

The 15 seconds it takes for another episode to play on Netflix is a huge waste of my time. #imamillennial

@k8Glav – 14 Aug

# I hate it when Siri doesn't listen and I have to get up and do things myself🙄

# Hear me out: We don't need bees, we have drones. Drones can pollinate flowers.

# HOW DID I GET TO THE POINT WHERE I CAN TYPE FOREVER BUT ADDRESSING AN ENVELOPE BY HAND MAKES MY FINGERS CRAMP?

@eyeseast – 3 Aug

Apple maps is down so now I have to stop at a gas station and buy an actual map...

@DoobieBrooks – 19 Jul

# Greatest fear? Accidentally deleting all my notes on my iPhone.

I just realized I lost my house key and my first reaction was to pull out my phone to try and call it.
#millennialmoment

# LEGITIMATELY DISORIENTED WHEN COMPUTERS AREN'T TOUCH SCREEN

@brookeleblanc – 26 Mar

I always forget to charge my Apple Pencil now I have to use my finger like a peasant.

@iamfelipa – 29 Jun

**\*BIRD SINGING SWEETLY OUTSIDE MY WINDOW\***
**ME: I DON'T KNOW THE SPECIES BUT ITS SONG WAS THE ALARM ON MY OLD PHONE.**

@FreddyRussell – 9 Jul

# It's come to the point that I feel weird not having my phone when I poop

Didn't even know it was British Summer Time because all my clocks go forward automatically

YOU KNOW YOU'RE TOO PLUGGED IN WHEN THE TRAIN GOES UNDERGROUND AND YOU PANIC BECAUSE YOUR BOOK MIGHT LOSE SIGNAL.

Someone needs to invent an app to tip people. Like valet or xmas tree guys. #imamillennial #ineverhavecash

@LauraNedbal – 2 Dec

The worst thing is hearing the ice cream man right in front of your house and only having your debit card

I ACTUALLY JUST TRIED PINCH TRIED PINCH ZOOMING ON A PIECE OF PAPER.

Watching bbc iplayer live but it's lagging by about 10 seconds so I can't tweet reactively enough about the election

@_alexandrakirk – 8 Jun

I AM SUCH A MILLENNIAL THAT MY PHONE ACTUALLY PUTS ME TO SLEEP AT NIGHT, WHICH GOES AGAINST SCIENCE...

# I cut my thumb while making dinner and it's seriously slowing down my texting abilities.

Bruh when our kids watch movies the 'cool kid' is gonna be vaping all the time #millenialtalk

'Hey, do you wanna see Spiderman vs. Vapeman?'

'I don't know, how about Planet of the Vapes?'

# #
# LYF GOALS

All I want is a cool job at a start-up in a beautiful city doing something totally worthwhile that doesn't take up too much of my time/energy, hilarious colleagues, working in an office with sleep pods, living in a penthouse with a pool, a super cute pug, zero roommates, three instagrammable holidays a year, a flamingo pool floatie snap, a personal trainer who is (not so) secretly in love with me, a playdate with Beyoncé and her kids and maybe an invite to fashion week every now and then.

I mean, is that really too much to ask?

**@Tatterasher reasons 2 b a mermaid:**

-No period
-No pants
-Perfect hair
-Get 2 lure men
 2 their deaths
-Plus a free
 clam bra

#ivanabeamermaid

@C_Bulletts – 17 Jan

Not only am I 23, single, and renting, but I haven't even fought in a wizarding war! #fallingbehind

@giacomo_bologna – 13 Sep

# I'M THE HAPPIEST WHEN I'M A UNICORN🦄... THANKS #SNAPCHAT ... #MAGICAL #MYSTICAL

@MsSunshyne216 – 12 Jul

# Where can I apply for a job as a Beyoncé historian? I'd fucking kill it, I swear to God. #lifegoals #beyhiveforever

@ElaCasati – 12 Jul

When I die my body will be dressed in Uniqlo, driven via Uber, from the wake hosted on Airbnb. #millennialgoals

**A KID IS WALKING AROUND THE MUSEUM SAYING ALOHOMORA TO EVERY DOOR, WHILE HER DAD PRESSES THE BUTTON SO IT OPENS IN TIME FOR HER. #LYFGOALS**

@NilupaYasmin  – 27 Aug

I strive for the intellect of Ruth Bader Ginsburg and the ponytail of Ariana Grande. #lifegoals

@kagb731 – 13 Jul

# I want to be so rich one day that I don't put my iPhone in a case.

# Wish it wasn't true, but playing The Sims is probably the closest I'll ever come to owning and renovating my dream home 🎮🏠

**Feeling really proud of myself cuz it's like 90 degrees outside and my eyebrows haven't melted off my face and I'R STILL on point.**

@ElbaFlamenco – 11 Jul

So before Facebook there was Bebo, and before Bebo there was MySpace, and before MySpace there was... what? Nothing?

How did people share their favourite memes? There were no memes either? WTF would people put in group chats if they couldn't communicate with memes, or gifs, or emojis? And WHY couldn't they Snap each other pug pics? There *were* pugs, right?

And you're saying music was a physical thing you could buy from a shop? And people went on blind dates without ANY way of digitally stalking them?

One more question... what's a 'fax'?

I honestly don't know who Bob Dylan is and I'm not sorry. #MillenialLife

Wow. I had to weigh and send a letter today at the post office and I just.

# Why, in 2017, am I having to send a fax?

Until recently, whenever my boss asked me to fax something, I'd just leave in the scanner, push a random button & pretend I did. #whatsafax?

# FEW THINGS CAUSE ME MORE ANXIETY THAN HAVING TO ACTUALLY MAIL A REAL LETTER

## #WheresTheSendButton

Just tried calling my Grandpa and got a beeping sound. Didn't realize that was still a thing. #busysignal

@shinn_hippie – 8 Mar

I hate when someone maybe 20 yrs older than me is like 'so anyway a VCR...wait do you even know what a VCR is?' #EyeRoll

@whoisapollo – 6 Mar

**COWORKER: 'CAN YOU FAX ME IT?'**
**ME: 'I'VE NEVER SEEN OR USED A FAX MACHINE IN MY LIFE.'**
**COWORKER: 'IT'S THIS EMOJI📠'**
**#OH #MILLENNIALPROBZ**

@MagicCJohnson – 6 Apr

Just saw someone with an iPhone 2g😧😂 #StoneAge

@A_Silv21 – 5 Jul

# Took about 15 minutes to send a fax today and not even 100% sure if it went through

# When you're phoneless and you've quit Facebook, I swear you can almost hear crickets chirping

CAN YOU HEAR ME?

@kricketchirps – 26 Mar

Waiting for regular mail, with no tracking data and no ETA almost feels...cruel, these days.

@annamarieDC – 17 Mar

# A BUFFERING VIDEO IS THE SAME FRUSTRATION OF A 90s KID IN THE BACK OF THEIR PARENTS' CAR LISTENING TO A SKIPPING CD.

@SleepieGirlie – 12 Jan

# 'PLEASE MAKE SURE TO TURN OFF YOUR PHONES AND TWO WAY PAGERS BEFORE TAKEOFF' #WHATSAPAGER ✈️

Having to pay for wifi in a coffee shop is our generation's version of not being able to watch color tv at a sports bar.

# when ur bestfriends phone is acting up, & text doesn't work, so you have to call her like they did in the early 2000s

# NOTES TO SELF WHEN IRL:

**1.** Noise cancelling headphones = I can't hear my fellow passengers, but they can still hear me. Expect death stares if you start to sing.

**2.** Avoid speaking in acronyms when around adults of a different generation. They won't get your clever irony.

**3.** Do not ask the busker if they accept contactless. You will get a confused glare.

**4.** Try to reference no more than two Netflix series in every conversation. You want to give the impression you *occasionally* go outside.

**5.** Not everything is touch screen. Do not pinch-zoom people's faces (again).

Never really know whether to chat to the other person when on an Uber pool #awkies

@c_ely – 19 Jul

I'VE NOTICED I'VE INVOLUNTARILY STARTED DABBING WHEN I STRETCH MY ARMS AND BACK.

@TheScottLloyd – 19 Jun

# Yesterday I sneezed so hard I broke my choker

I think one of
the greatest
tragedies
of our time
is in the
underutilization
of the jazz flute

@HeyJessBecker – 19 Sep

# To yoga retreat over Easter or not to yoga retreat over Easter.

At a restaurant wasting money on a drink because I need to charge my phone.

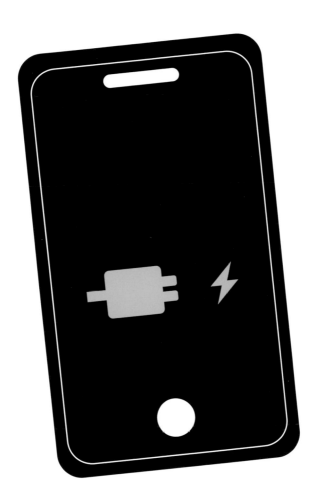

# I'M FINDING MYSELF ABBREVIATING THINGS NON-IRONICALLY ANYMORE.

@kelseyreres – 28 Mar

Since the whole 'pronunciation of GIF' debacle, I'm now questioning whether I'm pronouncing meme correctly #MillenialAngst

@ben_hart – 8 Jan

I roll my eyes so hard
sometimes I feel like
my retinas could detach

# THE AWKWARD MOMENT WHEN *NSYNC 'BYE, BYE, BYE' RANDOMLY COMES ON AND YOU KNOW ALL THE WORDS.

# Welcome tc your twenties: NOBODY KNOWS WHATS HAPPENING

**#wordsofwisdcm**

Many thanks to the authors of these tweets. Every effort has been made to credit tweeters; please contact the publishers with any corrections.